ADISHAA

SECRET OF THAT DAY

AADESH DUBEY

This Volume is dedicated to all

Who are part of this beautiful journey of life called love.

Contents

Foreword

I started out as an engineer and while doing the job in an IT company, i got excited about writing and creating my own work. We live in a society where meaning of love is different for everyone in my perspective love is everything it should be like one soul dwelling in two bodies.

This book provides a widely useful compilation of love, passion and how one person helps and nurture other in an relationship. This volume is an important resource for people who are in love. First it provides different perspectives of how people go to an extent to follow love of the their life because in a country like Indian its not allowed to get marry to anyone beside own religion and even from different caste this is what exactly seen in the novel love of an couple from different religion.

This book should be read by another who are in love and wants to see the magic of love because it offers a wide set of emotional ideas of deep affection, fondness, attachment. All the key processes for different changes in an relationship from being loving to seeing difficult time together.

Overall this book offers a variety of love perspectives and how a person get passionate and grows together as one soul.

PREFACE

This book appeared as a result of me being alone sitting in my room as this is the only time when an human being thinks in a deep manner that's what happened with me while noticing different people taking about love, walking hand in hand with each other, spending time with each other, after coming across all these I wanted to share what I have noticed and felt while observing things and people around me. I wanted to provide my readers a reflection of what I feel or what I felt.

This is my story. It isn't perfect but that's okay as nothing in this universe is perfect and whole. I hope it helps people to love more and feel more through my small reflection.

Acknowledgements

Writing and publishing a book is harder than I thought and more rewarding than I could have ever imagined. None of this would have been possible without my family members, their love and support always encouraged me.

I am grateful to my friend Akansha who helped me throughout this journey with editing process and guiding me in several stages of my work.

Furthermore, I want to acknowledge Notion Press for publishing my work and making my dream come true.

PROLOGUE

"Love is not a temporary feeling or emotion, Emotions and feelings change, Sometimes daily.
But true unconditional love is Everlasting".

And Fights are natural in any relationship. But what matters the most is the way you sort it out.It should not be about "Ego and Ignorance"

But about
"Love and patience"

I

The Previous Night

Curled in his arms, bedsheets were a mess that morning. Her hair stuck to his sweaty arms, his breath was caressing her ears, and she was smiling. Somewhere she knew, life is not going to be the same for her. She glanced at his calm and composed face and admired the perfect dusk of his skin. She moved her fingers over his face. She was creating a silhouette in her mind. She was too sleepy to open her eyes. And the best part was to stroke his eyebrows. She knew he would always smile when she does that. She would stroke his brows until he woke up. She knew that was the best way to say "Good Morning" to him. And that day, she wanted to do everything that she always thought about. Not just the way everything happened, there was something, something in their eyes, in their minds, and in their bodies that just took "them" a step ahead.

Thinking over the last few years wasn't something that came along with choices, instead, she had nothing but to keep up that one ray of hope that someday, somehow, she is going to fall in his arms. There will be a day when she won't be holding back anymore. The glimpses almost flooded her eyes with tears. Lying down with him the way she always wanted to, kissing him softly when he sleeps, moving her fingers in his hair, and grabbing them until he holds her tight. She was living the time of her life when everything that she had thought about was then a reality. She softly rubbed his cheek against hers and nuzzled her nose against his nose from the side.

He opened his eyes and looked at her. He smiled, and she blushed. He turned around and kept his face against her chest and held her. Held her like a small baby, as if he was never going to leave her. He held her with just the right amount of force and passion. He smiled within the ends of her curls and swiped them away from her face. He gave her one hard look and softly kissed her lips. Within a second, she fell into his arms as if she was so broken and tired as if what she was searching for have just found her with the same madness.

There were so many questions banging on her inner head, but she chose to let them be and not ponder over the things that would snatch her euphoria. It was her time to forget about the world. As the passion in his eyes gave away to his hands to caress her everywhere from head to toe, she could not resist but respond with perfect moans. She took his name with every breath and moaned even harder when she felt breathless. She couldn't resist the glimpses to scatter all over her mind as of what the last night have been for her.

THE PREVIOUS NIGHT

"Is there no light on your staircase ??" She said while climbing the stairs that would lead to her "Dream mansion".

"Ohh!! Aagghhh..." She cried. She stumbled onto the first step, perhaps because she was too naive to be able to understand where those stairs were leading to. But he held her arm, as to prevent her from falling.

"Miss, you're unable to walk on my stairs, how will you manage me and this house ???" He said and laughed softly.

"Will you just shut up...I will !!" She said in a baby tone and caressed her to where his stairs have just kissed her "welcome"

"And by the way Bhondu Ji!!. I'll save this bruise as a memory which will always remind me of this day". she said and looked straight into his eyes. The same dark liquid ink eyes she gets lost in from the day she started seeing through them.

There was a thing with him. Whenever she looked into his eyes, he was conscious. perhaps to avoid some secret silent decisions being revealed to her. Well, whatever that could be, it didn't matter. The important part was the "time" they were having with each other. Those desolate moments. Desolation from the world and the rationales, desolation from "this v/s that", "yes v/s no", and, from "you v/s me" for that matter, there was desolation from everyone and everything.

They weren't two people anymore. They were one!

As soon as she reached the door, she could hear him ringing the keys in his pocket. He took them out and asked her to open the door.

She looked surprised!!" Welcome to Your mansion highness". He said as she stepped in. She looked so surprised. Instead of looking at what this house had to offer Her, she looked at him. And looked at him with questioning eyes that already knows the answers to everything said unsaid. That was a moment when she felt like

embracing him and never letting him go. But is there anything that never ends?? Well, practically no. But then, she wasn't living the "time" practically and that was what felt like bliss. When you don't have intellect involved in a relationship, just remember one thing, that is the best one you have or ever had!

She hugged him and didn't let him go.

As it is said, everything has to end somewhere, somehow, someday! The embrace ended.

She looked at the house finally. It was a two-bedroom hall kitchen apartment with two rooms on either side, a little ahead, straight to the entrance gate there was a glass pane almost of the size of the wall. She moved towards it and removed the curtains. She was taken aback by the view it was offering.

"It's so beautiful!" She exclaimed like anything.

"Yeah...But not more than you" he said and laughed

"You mechanical engineers!! You don't even know how to romance a girl" she said, and he shrugged!

"So this left side room is mine. The other room remains vacant mostly. It's used only when my family visits me. Both the rooms have washrooms attached! Pick for yourself where you want to go. Everything is all yours" he said and smiled!

"Yours is mine...All. mine...But you go first and have a shower, I can't bear these sweaty sweaty arms...Till then, I'll look around and see the House ok" she said, and he left.

She looked around and find newspapers spread everywhere, water bottles left capless, books lying from floors to fridge tops, and especially the places they are not meant to be. She saw his clothes from the sofa to the dining table and where not!

He always claimed to be a very tidy person! She was in a habit of believing whatever he says every time, but she was witnessing the mess which was no different from any other bachelor's apartment! It was quite normal and in fact, she was enjoying cleaning the place off. She enjoyed it because she knew life is not going to offer her so many Moments where she would feel like his wife!

When he came back after 15 mins, he could see the actual neat person in the room. He was smiling to see that the books have returned to the shelf, and newspapers were folded and kept in the right place. He opened the fridge and saw water bottles filled and kept neatly. He was admiring what his life would be like with her! He was smiling and smiled for a little longer. She wasn't there when he came out. She was in the other room.

"Oh, God, I love her", He whispered and smiled again'.

"Aji sunte ho! Ap Apne kapde Kaise Kaise Rakhte Hain?? Yaha to bakheda Phaila hua hai??" (Listen, dear, where do you keep your clothes?) She called out from his room and laughed. He went inside and saw her struggling with a pile of clothes which she was so confused about where to keep. He came near the cupboard and took the pile from her hands.

"Have you come here to be a servant?? Let it be…Ye ho jayega" he said and closed one door of the cupboard from his side …

"Will your wife be your servant too?"

She said almost instantly.

He had nothing to say. But he knew exactly where the conversation was leading! They knew this one fact crystals clear from the day they were together!! They were two different Colors! How could they just mingle and give rise to a single color!! The color of humanity.

Her face dropped down as she said that!

He looked at her and embraced her.

"Look!! now leave all this, go and freshen up. You must be tired".

Finally, after a long wait of 20 mins, she came out. She wore a black dress that he gifted her on her last b'day! She always felt happy wearing it and she would keep smiling all the time. That dress!! It was a one-piece, and she wore it only with him! She had never worn that dress with anybody! She was waiting for that one day when she would wear it and show it to him. It was an off-shoulder dress, and he was watching her with his mouth wide open. She was blushing which was so contrary to what she is. She was a girl who cannot blush, who just doesn't know how to blush!! But that day, only God knows why she was laughing like hell!

"Now I am going to remove this okay? It's my b'day present! I don't want to ruin it", she said and stood up from the bed.

"Noooooo…Why are you changing? You're looking beautiful !!" He said dropping down his face!

"Yaa but I want to keep it safe … So, you'll have to agree ", she said.

Within an hour, they had their conversations, their little arguments over his alcohol and leniency towards studies, over her not-so-feminine looks, and everything they found important to be discussed. The last thing was something over which they both agreed.

II
The Big Day

Finally, the big day arrived. She had been preparing for this Holi party for the last so many days. Despite all the preparations that she had done with all her heart, she was nervous. And nervousness was quite obvious. She had been restless all this while for even the extremely tiny things which she had never been bothered about. She had been so reckless with her hair all her life but today she was so particular about every strand of her hair being straight. For the last 30 minutes, she had been in front of the mirror. She had plugged the hair straightener in and was continuously stroking her curls to get them straight. It was a tedious job for a girl like her who had never spent more than 5 minutes in front of the mirror. She decided to straighten them because the last night she had a conversation with Rishi which concluded that Rishi loved the straight hair on women.

Everything that Rishi ever uttered was crucial for her attire. She wanted to look just the way he wanted to see a woman. She wanted to be the only woman that Rishi would ever want to see. And to get close to him, she was trying her best. She knew she was already in his life. Text messages were doing their job well. Between those subtly romantic conversations that start from nowhere and end in nowhere, there was a different universe between them in 'nowhere' which they were enjoying with the deepest of their feelings. Surely, it was difficult to move ahead directly from where they were but, they were on the way to doing so.

Midway through her beauty treatments with eyeliner and mascara, she received a call from Rishi.

"Hello! Hey Hiii !!" A low infrasonic sound greeted her from the other end. Rishi had a good base voice, but he chooses to keep his volume low.

"Hiiiiii" ... A girl's Long Hiii means that she wasn't anticipating a call at the particular moment but she's glad to receive one.

"Ammm...Youuu...coming right?", he asked with a lot of hesitation which made it quite evident that even he was waiting for her.

"Yaa actually I was just getting ready. I'll take 30 minutes to be there." She replied gently. Her tone was as soft as her emotions for him. Too soft to get hurt even by a gentle stroke.

Love, in its initial few phases, is actually so fragile. Only the test of time can make it stronger. This doesn't happen overnight. It takes time. With them, it was growing in the same way and was soon to be tested.

"Ohh! Okay...So you'll be coming directly to the venue? Right!?", he asked again, this time with a little less hesitation in his voice.

"Yaa...probably. But why are you asking this?!" She doesn't let a single chance go in vain to tease Rishi.

He smiled at the other end. If phone calls were to tell the expressions, the phone would have been red by now. Because certainly, Rishi Gujral was smiling madly. And his tone mildly proved that.

"No! Actually, I thought you would come to Zuly's place before". He tried too hard to sound casual. If Aayat was the girl she was a year back, she would consider the sentence normal. Having seen Rishi blush, she knew he had to be too strong to not let his feelings come out of the mobile phone.

"What do you want? Shall I come to the venue or your place?" She said that bluntly. Without any hesitation or even a streak of being uncomfortable.

"Your call…" She hated this about Rishi. He would always let the final decision be on Aayat. Her neurons were busy thinking as to how she can reach his place. She needs to find a good excuse to be there. In any way, Zuly was going to be quoted this time too.

"I'll be there in 30 minutes…", She said and smiled.

"Where? The venue?", He bit his lower lip in amusement.

"Bye Rishi…". Finally, she laughed loudly.

There was no dilemma as to where she needed to be in the next half an hour.

The route to Rishi Gujral passes through Zuly Akram. She knew she'll have to call her once again and let her know that she was coming.

"Zuly! I'll be there in 30 minutes. Wait for me. We'll go together." She blurted out everything in one go without letting Zuly say anything.

"Ha ha ha ha…Someone's excited!!"

"Shut up! I'm getting late…I need to get ready."

She said and disconnected the call.

Within the next 15 minutes, she hurried up like anything. Later, she put on her earrings that she got a few days back with Zuly, wore a nice cologne, tapped a few times on her face to let the compact completely settle down and merge with her natural skin color, and put up her favorite matte brown gloss and let loose her hair and unleashed them to see how they touched her back. She thought of putting a small dolphin clip to tie them up but then she chose not to. Everything should remain unbounded today and so did her hair.

Finally, she grabbed her bag from the cupboard and ran out straight. She was wearing a bottle of green-colored Kurti with blue leggings and a dupatta with a combination of both colors. The theme for the party was Indian.

Minutes later, she rang the doorbell.

Zuly opened the door. It was such a shock for her to see her best friend look the way she was looking that day. Zuly knew that her friend doesn't know how to put on even a simple nail paint but today, the way she had dressed up was commendable. She could never imagine Aayat looking the way she was looking. Her jaw was almost midway, and she kept looking at her like that for a few seconds before Aayat entered her house.

"Will you let me in?" Aayat came inside.

"...Oh my God !!" Zuly was confused to say anything.

"How am I looking?? Tell me no" Aayat asked with such hope in her eyes to hear only good comments.

"Why have you put on so much makeup? Are you getting married or what? What have you done to your hair? And oh my God! Why are you dressed up so badly ?" Zuly was pulling her leg and she succeeded in doing so.

Aayat's face went pale immediately. The corners of her eyes started getting moist.

"No no!! Are you mad!? Don't start crying!! I was kidding yaar!" Zuly said immediately.

"I'll kill you Zuly..."

"You're looking, beautiful Darling! Rishi wouldn't be able to take his eye off you! I swear and I am not joking this time."

"Who said it's for Rishi? Are you mad!? You don't think twice before you speak. Why do you always bring Rishi in!?" Aayat said pretending to not understand anything.

"Ahaan! Really ??" Zuly kept looking at her face with questioning eyes.

"Okay come on now leave it. We're getting late. Let's go ." Aayat said and they moved out.

"Byeee maa...Come soon" Zuly bid bye to her mom and left.

"Bye aunty..."

"Bye beta...Enjoy yourself. I'll join you soon." Zuly's mother replied from the kitchen. Only her voice came out.

While going down the stairs, Aayat asked Zuly to check for Rishi if he was there.

"He said he'll go with us," Aayat said and smiled.

"Ohkaaayyyy!! Now I got it. Why are you here!?" Zuly laughed.

"No No...Shut up! You don't know anything ."

"Let's go then. He would be waiting for you, not for me." Zuly said and noticed a thin perk on Aayat's face.

Aayat rang the doorbell. And there he was.

Rishi looked at Aayat and for a moment he was still. They both looked at each other without any specific expressions on their faces. They were just quiet.

Rishi didn't say anything after that.

"Shall we go?" It was Zuly to break the silence between them.

"Yaa! Yess..." Rishi said and picked up his hanky from the table and moved out.

Zuly was smart to not walk with both of them and be "Kabaab mein Haddi".

She walked ahead of them. The venue was a walking distance away from there.

Rishi and Aayat walked together while Zuly plugged in her earplugs and moved ahead.

"I can't walk with such boring people like you. You people don't talk? How can you not? Well, I'll reach the venue before you guys. I am going. I'll see you there".

"No, wait." Before Aayat could say anything, Zuly moved way ahead with her earplugs to even listen to her.

"It's okay. Let her Go." He said in his calm and composed voice.

Aayat replied with a shy smile.

"Amm ... You're looking very different"

Finally. He's coming somewhere. Aayat thought.

Since the time Aayat met Rishi, she was waiting to hear some compliments from him but with Zuly on their side, it was not possible.

"Different... As in ?"

"As in ... Different!! Just ... Different ..."

Aayat looked at him disappointed with the answer.

"Hmm ..." She smiled fake.

Rishi knew Aayat wanted to hear more from him yet He was taking his own time to tease her.

The walk was quiet and surreal. She was hoping to hear something, at least something from him. But Rishi was equally prepared for teasing her with his silence. He knew she had done all of this hair and everything for him. Teasing Aayat was such fun! He was laughing internally.

"So when is your result going to be out ?" Rishi asked to break the silence.

"It's probably in the last of May. 28th of my 29th is the anticipated date."

After that, the whole walking expedition was quite like the atmosphere.

The day was cloudy and there was no sun to be seen. A nice gentle wind was blowing slowly and it was touching their faces. Aayat had to keep moving away from the strands from her face now and then. Rishi was looking at her silently and observing her little struggle with the wind. He could see the unhappiness in her eyes but he still chose to keep them shut. He wanted to appreciate her efforts at the right time with the right words at the right moment.

Good things take time to come.

They finally reached the venue. The gentle aroma of fresh Thandai welcomed them. Decorations were beautifully done. It was a park near the society where the welfare team decided to put up a little shade with colorful silver-mirror work dupattas. It looked like a small canopy. The pyramid-shaped decorations were giving a beautifuaestheticcs to the place and in between them, there were spaces from where the cool breeze was seeping in. In that long space, in one of the corners was the pot-bellied thandaiwaala. The entire bunch of young boys was covering him. Aayat could recall a few faces amongst them.

There was no girl near him initially but it was obvious that by the time everyone would be busy, even the girls won't miss out on Bhaang. Aayat was reluctant in going over there. She spotted Zuly sitting under the Shade of the last tree. She was with her childhood neighbor friend, Aastha. Aayat excused herself from Rishi and moved ahead to Zuly. Rishi just saw her moving away. He smiled.

"What took you so long Aayat. Where have you been !? It was just a 5 minutes walking distance and you're 20 minutes late". Zuly said and laughed.

She could see the color fade from Aayat's face. Aayat was not happy at all. Zuly was expecting a happy girl would come and then she would probably share with her what the walk had been like but there were no such expressions. She looked disappointed. Her forehead was covered with layers and layers of creases.

"What happened ?" She asked again.

"Nothing! Everything's fine." She replied in a dry tone.

"Where's Rishi ?"

"I don't know". Aayat replied roughly.

"Oh! I see! Did you have an argument or something with him ?"

"Why would I ? ... And you know what? You shouldn't have left me alone with him. I came to your place so we can come together, and you left me with Rishi !"

Aayat said, frustrated.

"Relax! Tell me what happened !? How would I find a solution otherwise ?"

"There's no solution. I just don't want to talk about it. Leave it. I'll go and meet everyone". Aayat said and left.

Zuly was standing there finding no reason for the change in her mood. She looked at Rishi from a distance. Rishi was wearing a white cotton kurta and blue denim jeans. He was with Vikram. Zuly moved towards them.

"Hi, Vikram!" Zuly greeted him.

"Hiii! How're you !"

"I'm good. But someone's not. What have you said to her She's so upset. Did something happen between both of you?" Zuly said, more to Rishi.

"M? No I did not say assaying to Aayat. What happened?" Rishi said pretending to be so unknown.

"Of course Of the course has done something. Otherwise, how

would you know that I am talking about Aayat? I didn't take her name." Zuly said and smiled naughtily.

Meanwhile, Aayat was looking at Rishi repeatedly and showing as if she didn't care. Rishi was noticing everything, but he was waiting for the right moment to say something to her.

Zuly called Aayat and asked her to come there. Aayat came half half-heartedly she wanted to).

Like Zuly, she too greeted Vikram.

"Hi, Aayat! What's up!"

Aayat simply smiled back.

Vikram looked at Aayat and then at Rishi. He was experienced enough to understand what was happening between them. Except for Aayat, all three of them were smiling looking other. Aayat was pretending to look away from Rishi. Failed attempts. After a couple of minutes, Zuly and Vikram excused themselves and left.

Rishi and Aayat were alone now.

Rishi looked at Aayat once again. This time, more closely to the disappointment in her eyes. Aayat saw Rishi with still hopeful eyes. As if she wanted him to say something and neutralize the past hour. Rishi smiled looking at her. Aayat couldn't understand the reason for that before, yet she smiled back slightly.

"Naraz ho? (Are you angry?)" Rishi said hoping to talk to her.

Aayat was quiet for a few seconds.

"No...Why would I be?" Her words and expressions were ways apart.

"Heyyyy!! Listen to me..." Rishi said turning his face a but todids towards were looking away from him.

"Aayat?? You're listening?"

"Hmm..." She said with a dropping face.

"Happy Holi Aayat", he said and picked up Red Gulaal from the table placed beside them. He stroked his thumb on her cheekbone and his fingers slid down her face making the whole of her right cheek red. He moved an inch closer to her and bent forward towards her. She looked at him, surprised. His fingers were still near her chin, looking straight into her eyes. The warmth of her heart was visible on her cheeks. They were burning. Everybody was busy with the celebrations, so nobody is them.

"Aayat!" Rishi said softly. "You look beautiful."

His thumb finally came off her cheek but the sensations of it were still there. Aayat has never been such a close pro it was the very first time she was feeling something like that. She did not know whether she was more nervous or shyer.

She started back at him and kept smiling. The last moment has become a memory for life. She had nothing to say. Everything was only felt.

The breeze was blowing even more and Aayat was having a hard time keeping her hair tied behind her ears.

Rishi moved his fingers and tucked the strand behind her ear. For a moment, her eyes were closed.

Away from them a few meters, Zuly and Vikram have been watching them.

"They look amazing together," Zuly said to Vikram while looking at Aayat and Rishi.

"Yaa! They do". He smiled.

"Mohobbat wehem deti hai, shikayatein bhi deti hai, Sawaal bhi deti hai...Do logon ke beech hokar bhi sar-e-aam Hoti hai...Itni Lazzat shayad hi kisi aur ehsaas mein ho... Awwal Awaal ki Mohobbat to aisi hi Hoti hai...Waqt lagta hai, us halke laal rang Ko pakka hone mein. Kai Aazma'aishon se guzarna padta hai, rishte Ko ghisna padta hai, Insaan Ko kharch hona padta hai... Aur uske Baad bhi ye yaqeen dilana na-mumkin hai ki agle pal ye saath rahegi ya nahi... Agle Lamhe mein ye teri hogi bhi ya nahi..."

III

You And Me

Well, it was biryani time.

She went inside the kitchen and began chopping onions!!

He had placed a chair near the entrance of the Gate of the kitchen and was talking to her. When she got finished with onions, he came near to her and hugged her from her back! She almost fell to the floor. Her belly would tingle even if he was just holding her and not doing anything !!

"Look!! If you'll do this, I am not going to cook" she said finally turning a bit of her face towards him.

"Then don't! Please..." His tone was serious.

"What are you saying?? Don't you want to have biryani!!"

"Not now, maybe later!!"

There was nothing left to be said. She knew she was not going to hold back anymore! She knew she will become weak in a moment and then she will forget everything, even her own identity too and the life she has left behind for a day!

He knew it, he will have to leave someday, maybe not today, not tomorrow but someday he will have to leave and even she is not going to stop him! Still, what was happening in a moment was irresistibly beautiful!

Her hands were entangled in his arms, the tension that was there between their entangled breaths, the chaos their minds have, gave a path for their bodies to be sorted! Minds were shunned, and hearts were beating out of their chest!

It was so musical how the clothes were falling from their skin to the ground! He initiated the kiss, and it grew passionate within a second! There was no disagreement. Even if there was, it wasn't strong enough to reach their heads! Magically his lips moved from her lips finding a way through her and then stopping to kiss her neck! He found her fears melting down from up the hills to the valleys of her neck and then moving ahead! She had his name written forever in her heart! Today, she could also see the hickeys out on her neck! His hands were perfectly moving everywhere as if they knew exactly the places, she wanted him to touch and explore! More than outside, there was an explosion inside which was violent enough to make them restless outside.

She was slowly dropped onto the bed. He was caressing her fears, her tears, and her soul. She wasn't in her senses ... The moment he held her close to his chest, something happened!! Something which she never experienced before, something which was loud enough to be heard all inside her nerves, something which was too deep to be comprehended by a naive mind!! She scratched his back and let him take over her!! He knew that their life is going to change!
And it's going to change a lot !!!
Minutes later, she found herself wrapped in his arms! A black quilt covered them below their necks! She was playing with his hands. Their fingers entwined! A truthful Silence prevailed in the room.

Breaking the silence was her voice ...

"Heyyyy ... I always wanted to ask you something". She said softly, stroking his eyebrows with her thumb. He was smiling.
"Yaa say"
"Why couldn't lord Krishna get married to Radha when they were so much in love?? ", she asked very innocently!

He cupped her face in his palms.

"You know what lord Krishna said...Marriage is the union of two souls. It requires two people...But I and you are not two! We are one!! So how can we get married!? Wherever I will go, you will be with me. You're not a different person for me. You are me", he said.
Tears flowed down her cheeks and rested on his chest. He kissed her smile.

IV
That Day

"That day" spreads its wings in my mind as I think about you today. We had a life without each other and now when I think about dying, you're the only person that comes to my mind. I walk these streets alone. I see nothing! nothing at all. There's desertion. Complete desertion. I thought I was doing what was right. Can I change this? Can I change what happened? Can I go back to you? should I even try to? can I look into your eyes again? will I be able to? these questions haunt me. I cannot sleep. I have grown insomniac. You're the only person I wish I could hold. Wish! I can only wish. I have never thought about spending the last days of my life alone. At least not without you. But it was me who has asked you to leave so I cannot escape the blame. And that is making it worse for me. Every day I come out of that place which I used to call home a few years ago, I feel a little alive.

That place haunts me. I know my words are futile today. There's no life in them. and you have all the reasons to perceive it as a lie. I don't know why I am writing this. Maybe writing all this will at least let me sleep peacefully. I don't even know if you will read this or not. I don't know if you will ever come to know that I am no more. Will you ever come back to this place? It was because of me that you left the city too. I thought I was doing it all right, but little did I know that I was slowly digging my own grave.

A flashback of the times that we have spent together is all I am left with today. I keep looking at your pictures on my phone and wish that if I could tell you how empty I am without you. Hindu mythology says that we come to this world seven times. I don't know. This life without you was nothing less than dying each day. And if the Hindu mythology is to be trusted, I wish that every life I get after this, I spend it in your shade. It's true, I am dying. And each day I am a step closer to it. Finally, it's going to end. This pain is going to end. I will be free. I will be in a better place. I am not praying for forgiveness.

No matter how many times I apologize, and how much I cry kneeling down on my knees, the truth is that I will never be able to overcome this regret. I will die with these tears of repentance. I am writing all this to you with no hope that you'll ever come to visit this place. I don't own you today. It seems like you are so far from reach. It seems like I can never touch you. I want to tell you that I could never replace you. I can never. There can be no one like you. Your place was yours. It still is. Today, I am dying, and I am happy that it's you that I belong. Even today I think about everything that happened. I try to find out the answers. What went wrong? Every day I used to walk alone on those streets thinking about you, hoping that someday I might run into You. It's just a dream now. A dream that I see with open eyes. A dream that makes these last days of my life a little less painful.

The trees surrounding this place are still as fresh as you are in my heart. The bench on the other side of the fence is covered with the same brown leaves. I remember how you used to collect them and keep them in your diary. "People put flowers in their diaries! and look at you? you put these dry leaves that nobody else even looks at." And what you said still echoes in me!
"Life is as fragile as these leaves are. We are so fragile. And just

a slight breeze is enough to make us fall apart. When I put these leaves in my diary, I feel that I am saving one life from breaking. As long as I can...not everything is under our control. Nothing is. We, as humans can only do so much! If we can spread a little love and warmth, surely, we will be at peace every day. I do it for myself, not for them"

" Mohobbat aur Zindgi, dono bezubaan hain...Ehsaas se Jyada aur kuch bhi nahi ... aur yahi unki khoobsurti hai ... jab tak kisi ki khamoshiyan padh kar samjh skte ho, zindgi bhi sirf tab tak mehsoos kar paoge ... Jis din be-his hokar sirf khud ke bare mein sochne lage to aapki apni zindgi kab shor machane lagegi aapko Ehsaas bhi nahi hoga ... Aur us din maut bhut Qareeb dikhai degi..."

V
Small Little World

"Mumm...AAAA Maggieeeeeeeeeee...!!!!", Mishti almost shouted this time. For the last fifteen minutes she was banging her hands on the table, ringing the spoons, and watching her favorite cartoon "Shin-Chan", and no wonder she learned so much from that character. Every time she sees Shimla Mirch in a dish, she just can't help but separate it. Last week she was crying because the Disney channel doesn't telecast "Action Kamen". Aayat came running out of the kitchen with a bowl of Maggie. Waves of hot steam covered her face. She could see the anticipation in Mishiti's eyes through the steam and how eagerly she was waiting for it. Her eyes lit up when she saw Maggie. As if she had seen Action Kamen and Shin-Chan live in front of her. Maggie and Shin Chan ruled her life. The way she smiles when she is surrounded by both can't be matched. What else four years old would find joy in?

"Presenting Maggieeee with a lot of cheese and no Shimla Mirch, just the way you like it, ma'am". Aayat presented her with a bowl of Maggie bowing down like she is presenting the crown of Queen Victoria. Mish Mustached wholeheartedly. Her laughter is something that keeps the house alive. And Aayat is fond of her laughter so much that whenever she is with Mishti she forgets that she ever had a life without her. Mishti completes her world. Indeed, mishit was her world.

Misti ate Maggie with full concentration over it. She was a chubby little kid of four. She just started going to school. She was no less than a blessing for Aayat. It won't be an exaggeration to say that if Aayat was alive today, it was because of Mishti.

Aayat loved her more than anyone in her life. Well, there was no one to be loved.

Aayat was a young lady, just 28 to be precise. The last 8 years of her life have molded her completely. As a young girl of 16, she was a stubborn teenager, restless all the time. She was one of those girls in her school and college who would be ready to fight all the time if she believes that her point is right and valid for the situation. She does that all the time. She would fight with people over everything that can be handled in a lot more ways other than just fighting. she would call her father every time just to tell him "Papa yaha about Grande log Hain… ye log insaan hi Nahi hai (papa these people here are inhuman !!)", and then cry over the phone with her mother on the other side and tell her how lonely she feels sometimes in the hostel. How much she misses being at home with her mom and dad. Raising her opinions every time was something she just can't resist. Even when she knew that her opinions always get her in trouble. She believes that if she cannot stand for the right thing, her life isn't worth living. Though the matters she always kept herself involved in weren't of life and death, she was typical about it. She wasn't the quintessential beauty of her college, but she had something in her. something which she was unaware of. As an emotional girl, she never saw life too seriously. She always found happiness in small things that people usually ignore in their race of life. She wasn't competitive about her looks. She never tried to "look good" like the other normal girls did. Her normal was weird for people. And she wasn't inferior about anything. That was the best part about her.

Her life was a little away from the realities in her bubble. Love knocked on her door very easily and she thought she got everything in her life that she can wish for. She was on top of the world. Though she was the eldest of the three kids in her family, she was the most pampered one. And the credit goes to her father!! Kid !! that's how her parents treated her. And she certainly hates that. She always thought of being the sincerest child of the family, handling every important issue with her father and she even did that. She was a blend of every color of the rainbow, yet she was unaware of it. Life is only beautiful when you don't get the reality checks, especially the way it came to her. She never thought her life is going to change upside down. Today, as a 28-year-old lady, she is beautifully elegant. A Bottle of green-colored kurta and a chiffon dupatta suited her like anything. She never forgets to wear a small little Bindi which looks like a tiny star on her forehead.

" Bindi looks so beautiful on you! It looks adorable. It makes me kiss you every time...your forehead baba" Rishi would tell her and laugh. It was some eight years ago. But his voice is still fresh in her mind. Every day she wakes up in the morning to his voice only. She feels that if Rishi wasn't there, she would never have Mishti in her life. Mishti was Rishi's gift to Aayat. And Aayat never misses a single chance to thank Allah for giving her Rishi, though it wasn't for very long, eventually, everything that happened in her life was only because of Rishi. In a way, her shifting to Dalhousie helped her move to a better life and she can never thank Rishi enough for that. Though Rishi was a very important part of her life, and he still is but she will never get back to him. She would never try to reach out to him.

"Wash your hands Mishtiiii and then touch anything!!"

She jumped out of the chair and ran towards the bathroom. It was 5 minutes to six. Mishti was on for a movie today. Shin Chan: Adventures of Hinterland.

Meanwhile, Aayat gave her hot chocolate, and there she was. In front of the TV waiting for Shin Chan to appear with his team. Mishti always has her hot chocolate in her sipper. She would open the bottle and swirl the straw every 2 minutes to check the levels. She was fond of chocolates. After shin Chan and Maggie, chocolates were next for her. She loved it but not more than Maggie, the cheese Maggieeee!!

Last month Aayat had to take her to a dentist. She had a bad toothache. The doctor told her to stay away from chocolates but when Mishti insists on one, Aayat had to give it to her half-heartedly. "Okay Okay!! I'll give it to you. but not more than half. And immediately after that you'll brush your teeth and go to bed. Is that a deal!?"

"Oooh!! okay, Mumma, I will. Now please give me one chocolate pleasseeee!!" Mishti would make a puppy face.

"Oyee !! cheater! we had a deal for half." Aayat would laugh at her naughtiness.

"Yaa Yaa half is fine. I thought of trying the other way!" Mishti winked and laughed.

Aayat can never say no to her for anything. It was their small little world with each other. And they were happy. Happy!!

While Mishti was busy watching Shin Chan, Aayat cleared the plates from the table. They were just two in the house, but the mess Mishti can create should not be missed. From her comics to her toys everything was in the best place according to Mishti. On the floor! Because she feels that whenever she wants to play or read her story books, her time should not be wasted on finding them and she should get everything lying on the floor!! Such an economical kid she was!

The doorbell rang and Aayat went to open to door. Unaware of what is behind that door waiting for her. There was some courier for her. She found no name on the envelope. It was after so long that she received some unofficial documents through couriers. Postal services have almost died down. She was thrilled to receive this in the last so many years. People usually prefer emails these days. WhatsApp messages killed the tradition of writing letters to loved ones. Nobody writes letters these days. They do wait for those double ticks to turn from grey to blue but have forgotten the charm of waiting for that one letter throughout the week. She was certainly happy about receiving one today. She could not find the name of the sender anywhere on the envelope. She signed the entry and the courier guy left.

While she was tearing the edges of the plain white envelope, she had a slight smile on her face. She finally opened the letter.

It was from Rishi!! Her mind went blank for a while when she saw his handwriting. There was nothing to doubt who was the sender of this letter!

Rishi Gujral was back!

The Rishi Gujral she knew of hates writing. He was someone who cannot even type more than 3 words if he had to reply. And in the last 8 years, he didn't try even once to reach her. It was as if she stopped existing for him. She tried calling him almost every day. He even answered the phone once or twice only to hear her cry. He had to pretend to be unaffected by her tears. He had to let her go. She wasn't strong enough to leave him and he knew that. He just had to. There was no option for him. And she knew everything. No matter how hard Rishi tried to be evil for her, she knew what lies in his heart. She knew him more than he knew himself. She knew why he was doing what he was doing.

"Why are you back Rishi? why? (Ab Kyun!!)" she mumbled to herself. She could hear Mishti laughing in the background. She turned around and looked at her. A moist drop of tear fell on her lips.

"Zindgi mein har rishte ka Aana aur Jana tay hota hai. Kaunsa Rishta kitne waqt Rahega hamari Zindgi mein ye bhi tay hota hai. Kabhi-kabhi pal bhar ke khwab jaise rishtein mein hum Apne Aap ko sarv kar dete hain... aur ye Bhool jate hain ki har cheez Aakhir khatm ho hi jati hai... Zindgi ke agle lamhe mein kya hojaye ye tak hamare hath mein nahi to phir hum kissi rishtein ki umar lambi hone ki shart kaise laga sakte hain... Takleef Rishta tootne se jyada hamara Jhoota yaqeen tootne se hoti hai..."

VI
The Letter

Locked in his room for the last 3 hours, he shuffled his cupboard to find a letter that Aayat wrote to him some 4 years back. It was not the only letter she wrote to him, but it was the last. The strange girl she was! In the 21stcentuary where social media have grown to become an obsession for people, she chose to write letters on birthdays, anniversaries, and every occasion that can be celebrated or cannot be celebrated for that matter. Rishi, on the other hand never paid enough attention to them. Hence, he had lost all those letters she wrote to him long back.

"When I won't be there to tell you that I love you and I am proud of you, my letters will." She said to him every time he complained about a long letter on his birthdays and New Year's. Though losing those letters doesn't mean that he didn't love her. He still does. He wasn't just careful enough to keep them. He was a man of the present. He never thought about the future. And this implied not only the relationship he shared with Aayat but also every other aspect of his life. She was the one who was concerned about their future. Like every other girl does in a relationship. It wasn't Rishi's fault for not thinking about the future especially when it came to the two of them. Their relationship could never be transformed into marriage. It wasn't so easy for a normal sane mind to understand.

The difference was in their names. She was Shaikh! And He was Gujral. Their names tell their story. They had the same skin, they wear the same emotions, and they carry the same blood, but they praised the one God differently. They knew everything yet they couldn't accept it. Especially Aayat. Girls are emotionally weak when it comes to accepting realities. They don't want to look beyond their comfort zone. They feel happy knitting the life of their dreams. That way, Aayat was no different. But the amount of love she possessed for him can never be fathomed by even Rishi himself. She knew it and after a certain point of time, he too accepted it

It was in the evening that he finally found the letter. He wanted to see the letter to smell of Aayat. She had this habit of spraying perfumes in the letters that she gave to him. Though there would be no fragrance in them today. He still felt something after touching it. He could feel the soft touch of her. He wanted to cry his heart out, but he doesn't have the energy. He has grown so weak physically and emotionally over the last couple of months. He could feel his bones moving inside him. His hair was falling rapidly, the body aches became adverse over the last few days. He kept awake the whole night staring at the plain walls of his room. Sometimes He would get out of his bed in the middle of the night and walk on the endless roads. He slept in the mornings when he could see some rays peeping inside his room through the curtains. He was scared of darkness. Humans are all ironic. The passage of our lives is nothing but irony. When we're in love, nights become friendly. We love them the most. We want to be alone all the time with our bright red blushing faces and that never-ending smile. We wait eagerly for the sun to fall. When his love was fresh even, he was like that. But now, he repelled nights like anything.

Humans love everything conditionally. For us, nothing is unconditional in the world, let alone love. Three days back he finally summoned the courage to write a letter to Aayat telling her about his condition and saying that he wanted to meet her one last time.

Yet he had already given up hopes to see her again. A part of him feels defeated already and a part of him knows that She still loved him and if she'll gets to know about him, she'll come running leaving everything behind. He hadn't told her about this because he knew she wouldn't have been able to handle it. She can't see the man she has given her life to die in front of her. She always prayed to die before him. She wanted to leave the world in his lap. Never in her worst nightmares, she can think of seeing Rishi die before her. He knew she can never stop loving him. Though all these years he only wished that Aayat falls out of love with him. But She pushed away his apprehensions with her unbound love.

The chilly evening breeze seeped into his lungs as he walked out of the back door. He sat outside his house in the backyard. He thought about Aayat. She was his constant thought throughout the days and nights. Whenever he is drowned in solitude, he sat out in the backyard on one of two chairs placed there. In the last few years, he has decorated his house the way Aayat used to dream about. He planted various saplings back in his garden and felt sheer joy in watching them grow. He had seen two phases in his life. First, When Aayat was with him, and second when he lost her. And in these two phases, he lived two completely different lives. With Aayat by his side, he has been a very materialistic man who would laugh at her love for dogs, her love for nature. He had told her many times to start seeing things practically and that he finds her very immature at times.

She used to feel bad about it that he can never understand her. But she always tried to make him see life with her unusual glasses. She believed that nobody can enjoy life as she can. When she left him, he evolved to be a different man. he started living life differently. And all this started because he missed her. The pain inside him flared rapidly and he had to find a way to let it out. He was an extremely introverted man and kept everything inside. Aayat was the only cave he confided himself in. When she left, he lost his control over life. Though it was his decision, he suffered equally as Aayat if not more. While losing her, he lost the only person he shared his feelings with.

So when he had to share his pain, he started doing things that she loved doing. He did everything. Wrote a diary, planted saplings, cuddled animals, watched old Hindi movies, listened to the old melodies she hummed, and started going to places he thought he could never approach. From old age homes to orphanages, he went everywhere. He read her favorite books and cooked whenever he recalled the first time she came to his house.

He asked her to make biryani. Whenever he sees biryani, he couldn't resist smiling. She would cook it, especially for him, and would secretly pack it to give it to him. She learned to make it, especially for him. Slowly, but steadily he stepped into her shoes and lived the life her ways. It didn't blot the pain away completely, but it was a beautiful escape, though transient. He would feel at peace for some time only to realize soon that he had lost her forever.

His phone had to give rings after rings to disrupt his muse.

'Vikram calling' ... the screen flashed his name.

"Bhai tu theek hai? (Are you okay bro?)" He sounded concerned.

"I am calling you for the last two hours. Where have you been? I was freaked out!" he continued.

"you don't have to freak out! what else could have gone wrong with me Vicky? more than this life, I have nothing to lose and I'm prepared for it ... don't worry, when I'll die, you would know "his tone was bleak.

"Stop talking like this!? I asked you to come home. I am coming tomorrow to pick you up" Vikram was doing what any ideal best friend would do. But Rishi didn't want to leave his house. He has stopped taking his medicines. Maybe he lost the urge to even think of living more. Vikram, on the other hand, was aware of his condition. He knew everything about him and Aayat. He has seen him grow worse after Aayat and he couldn't just leave him on his own now.

"Look! I don't want any arguments. Last time you said you'll think about it. That's why I didn't force you. Damn it! stop punishing yourself Rishi!! why the hell you don't understand? We are worried about you. Look I know it's difficult for you but please don't make it worse for yourself."

"Don't worry about me, Vicky. I wrote to Aayat about my condition. And if she comes in my absence, she'll be worried. I have to be here for her. At least this time. This is my last time. I can't ditch her. At least not now. This is the only time I can be with her. Perhaps this is the only time I have. I know you're concerned about me, but I am concerned about Her. I want to wait for her. And I know she'll come. She has destroyed herself for me, gave up her life which she could have spent like any other normal girl. But she waited for me. Now it's my time. It's my time to wait for her..."

"Unki Mohobbat bhut Aasan thi...Aam thi...Dusri mohobbaton jaisi, jis mein wahi khumar tha, wahi pagalpan, wahi khuloos wahi aarzoo wahi bebaak buland Aawaz, wahi lad jaane wala jazba tha ...sab kuch tha...sab kuch Aam tha phir bhi kitna kuch Khaas tha! Naam alag the, Rang alag the yahan tak ke Hausle bhi juda the ... Ek ka Zabt aur dusre ki Majboori, kiske paas kya kam tha? kiski Qismat kahan haari? Zindgi ne kitna kuch badal diya tha, kitna kuch cheen liya tha...Unka Rishta, yaqeen aur waqt ... jo nahi cheen paai, wo tha Ehsaas...Ehsaas Reh gya...kitni aasaan mohobbat thi unki ... Aur Itni aasaan mohobbat karna kitna mushkil tha..."

VII
Till The Last Breath

Aayat shaikh!

I never thought I would talk to you ever again in this life. I say this not because I hate you. I can never hate you. How can I? I am afraid of your hatred. "Tum naraz hogi mujhse bhut naraz", I know. and you should be My decisions have been a reason for your misery. I never wanted this. I swear I never. Do you know why I couldn't contact you all these years? Because I had nothing to say. I thought I will never show you my face again. I didn't know how I would look into your eyes I have been the reason for your misery and now when I am thinking about seeing you again, I didn't know what I say to you. You know I am bad with words.

You know I could never express myself. It was you who would read stories my eyes. I couldn't get another Aayat Shaikh! and honestly, I didn't even try for it. Aayat, when you left, I thought I was strong enough to bear a separation. I thought I was practical and that I could move on in my life. But I couldn't. I just couldn't. I don't know. I thought I was playing my cards right. But God has some other plans for me. Aayat, do you remember we argued once over a book by Duroy Datta which was supposedly your favorite at that time?

"Till the last breath", where the protagonist "Pihu" was suffering from ALS (Amyotrophic lateral sclerosis). You made me read that too because you wanted to share your pain with someone. After all, Pihu died and Arman was alone now.

"Jab do logon ki ek mohobbat se koi ek chala jaye, to dusra zinda kaise rehta hai? Kyun wo mar nahi jata?"

you said and as usual, I laughed at your stupidity of taking stories too seriously. And after that, we fought over who is going to die first between us.

And when I said "I wish I die of cancer" out of being humorous (stupid though), you started crying. You must be thinking about why I am telling you all this today. I am saying this because I want to tell you that God has accepted my wish. I am dying, Of cancer. No, I am not kidding. Please don't start crying! I have always been afraid of your tears, and you know that. I had only so much time. I want to see you once! please ..it's been years since I saw you. I have your pictures on my phone and I see them some thousand times a day. But before I end this life here, I wish to see you. I haven't changed my address. I haven't changed my phone number. If you feel like meeting me, please come back to Delhi. Or if you allow me, I can come there. I just want to meet you. I won't take a lot of time. And I promise I won't disturb your life this time. This is probably the last time I am going to distress you. Perhaps the last time I could be with you. Let me take this one last memory with me. Please!

(Aayat Shaikh!! Mein tumse na milne ke Daawe karta tha...aaj dekho! phir tumhare dar par khada hun... bina kisi jhijhak ke. Kyun ki mein aaj bhi tumhe khud se itna hi qareeb mehsoos karta hu ... Mein Janta hu mein aaj bhi tumhare saamne Besharm ban Sakta hun .Aaj bhi mein tumhari mohobbat par sawaal nahi kar sakta ... Mein tumhe zindgi mein kuch nahi de paaya magar Na jaane kyun mujhe pura yaqeen hai, tum meri ye aakhri khwahish zaroor poori karogi...Tum to hamesha se aisi ho na...)

Love
Rishi (Your Bhondu)

That one letter she was excited about a few minutes back has shaken her world completely. The ground beneath her feet had slipped away. The nerves in her body froze down. She couldn't feel the blood inside her. She couldn't believe the letter. Did he just say that? Is he going to die? Rishi! Rishi Gujral, the person In whose name she has written her entire life is going to die?

She thought someone might have sent it by mistake. But the name on the letter, the handwriting, that fight over the book which only she and Rishi knew about?? Everything just can't be a mistake. After so many years, why would he write about his death to her? The questions in her mind were logical, but her heart didn't want to entertain them. She still wants to believe that he didn't mean what he had written...Rishi Gujral is dying?? How can he just die?? Though he has never lived with her virtually he was always there for a moment everything around her went blank.

She couldn't even cry. Her tears seemed to have dried up. She roamed around the house lifeless like a zombie. She looked at the photo frame placed on the side table beside her bed showing the last picture of both of them together. They were looking at each other. It was a candid picture. She looked at it for so long. She had to look away when her eyes started hurting. A hot rush of tears came out of her eyes, and she cried like a baby. She couldn't hold them back anymore. She looked around and saw Mishti sleeping on the sofa in the living area. Mishti didn't know what Rishi is to her. She was too tiny to understand this web. She did ask Aayat about the photo frame, but Aayat could only tell her that the person with her in that photograph is a cherished old friend.

"Mumma, when will we meet your friend? All my friends at the school meet their relatives and friends who would bring chocolates for them. Will your friend also bring me chocolates? The Cadbury,

milky way, KitKat, and Yess Oreeeoooo Silllkkkk...Yummmmm...??"
Mishti would ask these questions very innocently. Aayat finds no
answers to her questions. She would come up with something to
distract her.

How could she tell her that if Rishi had been here, he would have
loved Mishti as no one else would? A father can be the clown for his
baby. He can do anything for his child. She would think about the
time when Mishti would start asking about her dad. What will she
tell her? How will she tell the truth to Mishti? And if she finds out
from somewhere that Rishi is her father, how is she going to react?
Will Mishti leave her too? She would want to spend her life with her
father

How would she react to Aayat when she'll finds out about the about
of their life? Which was so complicated! Those questions became
a reason for her distress because she received a letter after 5 years
from Rishi which said that Rishi will be no more. How would Mishti
react when she'll find out that she had a father she could never live
with, and he died of cancer? She would start Hating Aayat. She,
like any other child, has the right to know about her father. She's
growing up. Soon she'll be a big girl enough to understand things.
Children these days are 10 years ahead of their age. Mishti was
indeed an inquisitive child. She anyways had several questions to
ask. How's Aayat going to deal with the situation then?
Now when she knows about Rishi, she couldn't decide whether she
should tell Rishi about Mishti or Mishti Rishi. In her head, she had
wronged both! Rishi didn't know he has a daughter and Mishti
didn't know about her dad. Aayat, on the other hand, knew
everything. She knew both sides because she was the only link
between them.
She went outside and sat on the ground near Mishti. She held her
hands and kissed them. She cried her heart out.
Mishti was in deep sleep. Aayat's sobbing didn't wake her up.
What have I done to deserve this? What do I do now? How would I

tell him about Mishti? He would hate me! I can't take his hatred! I have kept a father away from her daughter! And knowing that her father is going to die is making the situation even worse. This feeling of guilt is overtaking my mind. But I had my promises. I could never break them! I promised someone that I will never let Rishi know about Mishti. But what do I do now? Even if I may not want to tell him about her, I might have to. I never felt more helpless in my life. Had I not kept those promises, Mishti wouldn't have been with me today!

She was consumed in her thoughts. That one grief of leaving Rishi years back was very difficult for her to overcome. She went through severe depression after that. And now this mere thought of seeing Rishi die is choking her. She didn't know how she is going to deal with the situation.

The tears have smudged her kajal. Mishiti's hands were all wet with her tears. She sat there till Mishti woke up.

******

"Yaaaay!! Holiday Holiday Holiday !!" Mishti clapped her hands and did her favoufavoritey dance. The same evening Aayat told her that they were going to Delhi for vacativacatione then, Mishti just couldn't stop smiling. She was very happy. She thought her mom was taking her off on vacatiovacationl go ghoomi ghoomi !!" Aayat had to pretend to be happy for a while when she was telling Mishti about it. She didn't know for how long she was going to be there but one thing she had decided before she made up her mind to leave for Delhi that was, she would tell Rishi everything about Mishti. As four years old, Mishti might not be able to understand this. But Rishi? She decided to tell him. Everything that happened 5 years ago. Of course, he had the right to know about her daughter. He's, her dad. And she is nobody to keep a daughter away from her dad. She was already submerged in the guilt of keeping them away for so long. She couldn't bear to have more.

"Mumma hum Kahan Jaa Rahe hain?? (Where are we going,

Mumma?)"

Mishti asked her when Aayat was packing her bags. Mishti was helping her by unfolding the clothes she had already packed in, to accommodate her teddy bear of her. "Tiger" she called it. She can't sleep without her "Tiger".

Her face turned pale when she heard Mishti asking that.

" Beta we're going to Rishi's uncle's house." She barely managed to get this one sentence out. Aayat couldn't look into her eyes. Though Mishti cannot understand what stealing glances means.

Slowly inside, Aayat was sinking. She could feel whatever little life she was left with moving out of her slowly. Since she got the news from Rishi, she hasn't been able to think clearly. The only thing she was clear about was that she is going to meet him. Keeping the promise aside, she had to let him know.

******

The flight arrived on time. This is it. She was coming to Delhi after 5 years. Her family was in Delhi before they got settled abroad. Her brother and sister were now in the UK. Her mom kept calling her but she doesn't want to leave India. Perhaps because leaving the country would mean leaving Rishi too. Dalhousie and Delhi aren't that far from which gives her a sense of calm that she isn't far from Rishi physically. The scorching sun of May was shining upon their head. Delhi welcomes people with pollution and humidity. Nothing changed. It was the same Delhi she had left a few years back. She completed a bachelor's degree in Medicine, the famous and wished-for undergraduate course MBBS. She had spent a lot of years in Delhi.

"Mumma ... I'm hungry (Bhukh lagi hai...)" Mishti drooped down her face and placed one hand on her tummy to show how hungry she was. Though she already had noodles and sandwiches in the front. But she was hungry !!!

Aayat, on the other hand, wanted to meet Rishi as soon as possible. Delay of A even a second was hurting her. She bought a packet of cookies and can of a juice for her which she munched on the whole taxi journey from the airport to Rishi's house.

Rishi lived in Hauz Khas Village. The taxi driver didn't know the exact location of his house. Aayat had to give him directions. Around 3 in the afternoon, she reached his house. She was standing out of his door and was holding Mishiti's hands tightly. It was not for Mishti, it was for her. She was scared. Too scared to even ring the doorbell.

"Mumma presses bell an ..." Mishti said and disrupted her muse.

She had to gather a lot of courage to ring the doorbell. Her hand was shivering. She finally rang the bell.

Rishi opened the door and saw Aayat standing right in front of him. For a while, he couldn't believe his eyes. He thought he was daydreaming about her. Even worse. He has grown schizophrenic. It took him five seconds to register what was happening around him. Aayat looked at him without blinking an eye. She had no expressions on her face. She tried to pull a smile to her lips. Failed attempts.

"Hello, Rishi Uncle". A childlike voice grabbed his attention. He looked down at Mishti. A tiny little girl wearing a blue skirt and white top, her hair was tied up to make two ponytails that perfectly landed up on her ears. To him, she looked similar to Aayat. He bent down and sat on one of his knees and kissed her cheek.

Though Rishi was taken aback having seen that little girl with Aayat that was not what concerned him at that very moment. All he could see that was Aayat was there. And She was there for him. He knew it.

He smiled looking at Mishti.

He smiled because Aayat was there.

He smiled, for the sun above his head finally shined brightly...

"Zindgi ka har lamha itna Aasan nahi hota ... Kabhi kabhi ek lamhe mein hum khud Ko kho dete hain, aur kabhi kabhi, aise hi kisi Anjaan Lamhe mein, Humein phir jeene ki wajha mil jaati hai ... Zindgi mein aise mauqe bohot Kam hote hain, jahan ye Dono Lamhe hum ek saath mehsoos kar paayen..."

VIII
Dear Diary

6 years ago,

December 2019, Delhi

"No...You have to see this ..." Zuly prompted her to see the fashion magazine she was reading since morning. Dude! "Look at her lashes – the smoky eye make-up, Oh my god!! It's so amazing" Zuly was going insane after that Fiama magazine she got from her friend in school. She was telling Aayat to investigate it and waste her time exactly the way she was doing.

Aayat heaved a long sigh, frustrated. Since morning, Aayat was on a racetrack! She kept her revision crisp and now it's been the second time she was solving the questions in the chapter "Constructions". She hated constructions with the deepest feelings. Anybody who would have seen her struggling with the compass failing at her rigorous attempts to curve a perfect triangle – she was hilarious at it.

Zuly's voice was blurred in her head, and it was fading away slowly. But when she grabbed her hand to show her the magazine, she cannot resist the expression on her face.

"These fashion magazines aren't helping you out tomorrow, you see. We're still left with 3 more chapters to revise. And you haven't touched your books ever since. I hope you know what that means right? Do you want to fail?" Aayat sounded a bit exasperated because Zuly wasn't interested in studying. And those two were gathered at Zuly's house for group studies and that too in the last lap – Bad idea. Not that she didn't know she was going to do well in her exams, but Aayat was freaked out to see her best friend paying no attention to the books she has kept open for the last 4 hours. It wasn't her fault though. Studying with Aayat was quite a pain in the ass.

She never let the other person breathe. With her, it's always more chapters — if you're done with math, great then pick up English and revise those 3 chapters that you have done a week ago. She wanted to beat everyone, from her schoolmates to her coaching mates to the other students of the other branch of her school. It was her wish to see her name printed in white on the big brown merit board of her school...Aayat was studying for her pre-boards, and unlike other students, the marks r to her. She cannot bear to not score well in any set of exams that she undergoes. Although everybody else was relaxed because for them pre-boards were just mock tests that prepare you for board exams, Aayat studied as if she was going to give boards the next day.

On the other hand, Zuly was least bothered. Exams were never stressful for her. She was a chilled-out girl of 15. Too young an age to be serious. She and Aayat were split personalities. They were of the same age, but Aayat was way more serious than her. Aayat was the kind of girl every mom wants to be a mother of. She was excellent in academics and religion too. Zuly's mom was fond of her, and she kept taunting Zuly with Aayat's examples – look at Aayat. she is so well behaved. Her clothes are so appropriate, that's how girls should be dressed. See, she wore a hijab also during the month of Ramadan.

And look at you! You never have time for anything apart from your nail art and what not!" Zuly was sick of these comparisons, but she never let those comparisons hang in between her and Aayat. That was a very rare quality about her. Aayat was a simple girl studious, and bold.

She was the eldest child of her family. And being the eldest one in the family comes with a lot of responsibilities. Every other person keeps an eye on you, what you are doing, what you're not! Who you meet, what you eat! Everything. And it's the responsibility of the eldest kid to be careful all the time. Though it wasn't difficult for Aayat to be that way, still it did piss her off sometimes.

"I'm giving you the last 15 minutes and after that, you'll start with mensuration – I can see that your geometry part is pretty good, but you suck on calculations. We need to work on that". The way Aayat used the word 'We', it was as if she was responsible for Zuly's result. Deep inside, unknowingly, she felt responsible for the people she loved.

Aayat flipped through the pages back-to-back to see what else is left for her. But she couldn't find any. She was done with the whole NCERT textbook along with some important parts of the help book she was using – RD Sharma. It was the most widely read book for math in class 10th.

She folded the pages carefully and made self-notes as to which set of problems annoys her the most. Like any other girl, she had a very peculiar love for Biology. She studied math because it was a part of their syllabus. Girls have a soft corner for biology, and they are very confident about it. Similarly, Aayat loved it too. It was her favorite subject not because it talks about a lot of things that students generally enjoy reading the most. Perhaps she was obsessed with the meticulous organization of the human body, how the bones are formed, how the blood is circulated throughout our body, and what arteries and veins are involved! Reading about diseases was her hobby. She would Google out some 3-4 diseases and then search for the reasons symptoms and cures. She would look for journals, interviews, and any smallest piece of paper that would give her some sort of information. Keeping the scraps with her and those newspaper cuttings brings elation to her.

For kids of her age, Biology is a subject that makes it legally authorized to read about the things which you hesitate to when you're a kid. The growing urge to know more about what lies within the cryptic systems down there in our pants is very evident and quite normal too. While boys drag an entire conversation about it to laugh out loud in the class, girls settle for tiny giggles now and then. Aayat have already studied the details back in her 8th standard when she stumbled on to the chapter "Reaching the age of adolescence".

Her biology teacher didn't teach the chapter because she felt the students already knew way more than what was printed in the books. Aayat had serious knowledge about the subject which was obtained from serious sources on the internet and not what people search for in incognito modes. When she came across this chapter in her 10th standard in a little more detail, she was happy because finally the subject teacher would have to teach the chapter and she can't skip it this time. This year, the kids were going to give boards. To make them aware of the subject, not in the crude laymen's language, but crisp scientific terminologies, she taught it in the class. Aayat had different sorts of questions altogether. She learned too much to get entangled in her questions.

Her biology ma'am could do nothing but smile at her. She was the apple of their eye. Teachers loved her. So, when she brings the most insane set of questions in the class, she wasn't scolded. Her ma'am took out separate time to make her understand why keeping the baby in a scrotum is not possible. Why can a father not be pregnant? Why the scrotum is invisible in a kid but visible in an adult male?

In one instance, during the same lecture, suddenly, she forgets where the scrotum is present in males. She was an extremely bold girl. Like those, who would learn science, the way it should be – with all the whys and how's. She didn't hesitate to ask her teacher where the scrotum was present. "But ma'am how can a scrotum be visible in an adult male? It is inside the body near some large intestine right...Umm, I think I forgot?" The whole class burst out in laughter and Aayat kept looking at their faces, pissed off at such an absurd gesture. She looked around and said loudly – "what's so funny ?" And everybody laughed even more at her stupidity.

"Class!! There's nothing to laugh about. about", Miss. Purva scolded the class.

"Aayat...Listen to me. You remember I told you that testes are descended from a male's body for regulating the temperature. Sperms cannot thrive at normal body temperature. Remember ?"

"Ohh yes, ma'am...Now I got it. I forgot." Aayat replied with a smile.

Sitting in the deserted corner of Zuly's room, Aayat was scratching her head on stumbling over some weird questions from the same chapter.

"Zuly! I cannot fix this problem. Can you solve this for me?" Aayat called out for her for the third time. It's difficult to seek attention from Zuly when she is painting her nails.

"Man! If you can't solve it, I definitely can't." Zuly said throwing her hands up in the air to show how repulsive the idea sounded.

Zuly was good with the subject. She was an ace at math. She always scored the best in her class.

"Listen to me now! I have some more questions. I think we should call Zahir Sir. He would probably ask us to come here, and we can solve it then. We still have time". Aayat said desperately. Zahir Sir was their math teacher in the coaching institute.

"You're done with your textbook dude! And if you can't solve some distant out of the syllabus questions from the other books, it doesn't matter. Nothing is going to be asked from this section. So, chill." Zuly said continuing to brush her nails.

"I don't think so. I spotted a similar question in the 2005 question paper. And questions are repeated now and then, we know that very well. I don't want to take a risk and feel guilty about it later." Aayat was adamant this time.

"Don't start crying now. Let me see." zuly lifted the book and began flipping the pages. Probably the first time that day.

Meanwhile, Aayat was noticing her facial expressions and hoping she would agree to go where she wanted.

"So I presume you either have no clue about it, which brings us to a dead end only Zahir sir can take us out from."

Aayat said straightforwardly.

"I gave up even before I peered into the depths of this. Woah! So many algebraic terms all at once. Looks like an unlimited buffet of unwanted dishes...I have only learned to kick out one value of X. Neah! Not my type." Zuly pushed the book away and rested her spine on the pillow behind her back.

"Let's meet Zahir Sir and get it sorted. Come on let's go" Aayat almost lifted her boo and pretended to leave the place as soon. Zuly finally pulled her down from the elbow.

"I don't believe this. You are so crazy. You'll go all the way to the other end of the zone to get these questions solved. On Sunday? Like really?" Zuly sat there in disbelief.

I don't want to go to the other end of the zone. I just want to go next door. Tell me you're taking me to Rishi. Aayat thought.

"Going all the way to the other end of the zone is our last resort" She chuckled glancing at Zuly's face.

"If it's really so I'm, we can surely ask RJ to do it," Zuly said.

Yess!! That's it. Yess had a neighbor who lived next door to her. Rishi Gujral. Rishi was initially RG for her but when swag took over her vocabulary, thanks to her peers in school, she started calling him RJ.

"No Zuly. We cannot. He is so busy. We can't ask for his help. I don't feel it's right." Aayat was reluctant about it. Perhaps because She hardly knew Rishi. The last time I last met him was at the new year's party in their locality. Zuly's place was surrounded by a bunch of cool neighbors. In cheerier neighborhood was very friendly.

On every occasion be it Holi, Diwali, Christmas new year, or Eid every occasion was celebrated with the same zeal and Enthusiasm. Aayat enjoyed it a lot. She could recall Rishi's face from the last time at a party. It was the first day of the year and at the special request of all the kids, the supervisors decided to bring in the DJ too. Contributions were done by each family. Aayat being Zuly's friend – Best Friend knew everybody well. Rishi's family was closely acquainted with Zuly's. Their families shared a very good bond. Zuly's and Rishi's mothers were like sisters. Rishi knew her since her childhood. They both have grown up and shared a beautiful virtual Rakhi bond. Every year Zuly Ties up Rakhi on his wrist and Happily, Rishi takes out her gifts awkwardly wrapped in the gift-wrapping paper.

"I know him too little to knock on his door and on ask for help. What would he think of me? A strange girl walking into his house and asking him to solve a stupid question." Irritated Aayat looked away.

"So you admit the questions are stupid," Zuly said and laughed alone.

"I'm seriously not up for this Zuly. I'm worried and you know how it is for me". Please for heaven's sake yar !"

When Zuly wished to do something, she did it anyhow. She had great persuasive skills.

Minutes later both were standing outside Rishi's house.

"RJ!! How long had you been sleeping?" Zuly shouted from outside Rishi's gate. She banged the door when nobody opened it after the first few bells.

Finally, the Door hissed open. A sleepy boy came out rubbing his eyes.

"Tu kabhi Aaram se nahi aa sakti kya?"

The boy said trying to open his groggy eyes.

"You sleep the whole day? Do you realize that? Whenever I ping you or come here, I always find you sleeping. Tell me! Have you been hibernating?" Zuly said making herself comfortable on the chair lying there in the living area. She pulled another chair for Aayat and signaled her to sit down.

Rishi ignored Zuly.

"Hi, Aayat" A familiar sleepy voice addressed Aayat which established her existence for the first time in the room.

"Hiii" Aayat replied generously.

"It was not me who wished to disturb your blissful sleep, it was her." Zuly pointed out to Aayat and took out a water bottle from the fridge lying there.
yet stared back at Zuly and then looked at Rishi's face briefly. He was staring back at her. Aayat was conscious around

Aayat was not the girl who depicted the characteristics of a girl. She was more like a tomboy. Unaware Unwakeful the features she owned. She can set anybody, which means a guy to fire if she finds out he is even thinking of looking at her that way. She never dated anybody even in her school. Nobody either proposed to her or offered her as it was called then. However, her male friends outnumbered her female friends always and she told this to everyone very confidently.

Her voice never grew bleak with any other guy. But when Rishi was around her, she always felt a certain level of hesitation deep inside her which even she was unaware of. Her body language, the way she talked, and the way she wanted to behave went all in vain when Rishi was around. When he was around her, she was guided by her unconscious mind that would make her heart race so fast that she can almost feel it coming out of her chest. It would cause some strange vibrations in her head and because of that maybe, her cheeks turned pink. She experienced everything without being aware of it and that was the best part about her.

"Yaa tell me what happened?" Rishi asked politely. This was his usual tone. He wasn't hyperactive like Zuly. He kept quiet most of the time and prefer to time as minimum as possible. He hated noise like anything.

"Zuly dragged me here. I didn't want to disturb you. I'm sorry that we woke you up. Amm, we stumbled on some questions which we are unable to solve. Zuly said you would solve them for us. I didn't want to come here. She pushed me and got me here. I'm so sorry once again" Aayat blurted out everything like a small child.

Rishi was smiling at her continuously. Probably he was smiling at her.

"It's okay Aayat. So many explanations just for coming here?" Rishi cut the long explanations short.

Rishi was a third-year mechanical engineering student. His college was located at the distant end of the city from where another state started. Noida. He rarely went to his college. Mostly he stayed at home and worked from there. He had two sisters, his mom, his and dad. These people were his family. Unlike Zuly, his financial condition wasn't sound. Working the whole day out wasn't really ng he did out of choice.

He taught kids s himself was in He also Gave home tuition to give, and this would add up to the required expenses of his family. He was fore youngest of the three. His eldest sister, Shikha worked for an IT company. The one 2 years elder than him, Chavi, was doing her graduation and she was in the final year. His father owned a confectionery shop, but it was mostly submerged in losses. Prakash's Uncle could not do much for his family financially. He always remained at a distance from his family, especially his son. The two never got along with each other.

He came inside and washed his face to get freshen up. Splashes of cold water on your face on a winter evening are dreadful. He muffled in his white DKNY sweatshirt and came out. He looked amazing to Aayat. Bearded Dusky face, Dark black liquid ink eyes glaring back with deep sadness. He was one or two inches taller than Aayat. He was the most appealing guy that she ever come across.

He solved the dangerous-looking entity with so much ease. Well, it was his subject. He chose math willingly.

"you both weren't applying the theorem which was given at the back of this exercise. It was quite easy." Rishi said giving the pen back to Aayat.

"Yes. She didn't. You should have applied the theorem Aayat!" Zuly brings in her flavor in everything.

"What! You should have even tried to pick up a book. You haven't studied a word since morning". Aayat smiled.

"Tu padh le. Tujhe fail hona hai kya ?"

Rishi said glancing at the least bothered Zuly.

"Well, these types of questions are easy. Don't worry." Rishi said glancing down at the books, avoiding direct eye contact with Aayat.

"Well, they are easy for you! I stumble at math's rad. I'm pathetic at it." Aayat said looking at him finally. Rishi smiled at her.
Q "Don't worry you'll do good. All the best." Rishi said turning the book with his anyways bleak smile.
There was something in his smile. Something that made Aayat feel differently about him. Aayat was under-confident about her exam the next day but when Rishi said "you'll do good" she felt it beneath her skin. He exchanged with her not only his smile but also his motivation. Motivation is to achieve what is unachievable.

Aayat went home and like her usual routine, she began jotting down the specifics of the day. Hers was not very difficult to know.

Dear Diary

I felt such deep silence in his eyes that it was almost impossible for me to look away. In a moment, I am weak. All I want to do is look into his eyes and seep in through the sadness it bears. I don't know anything about him. All I know is that He seems to be such a nice and genuine person. Even today, I could have solved the questions alone but then I chose not to. I wanted to meet Rishi. Ever since I have seen him, I always wanted to have a conversation with him. You know how I feel about certain people. And Rishi is surely one of those. I had to prompt Zuly to take me to his place. I couldn't tell her that I wanted to meet him. Now that I have, I know he boosted my morale so morale times and I can now surely be confident about what I know. He is not aware of my life, neither and I am. But one thing is for sure we certainly have innervated bond which hasn't been defined yet. I hope he smiles at least once tonight before he sleeps.

Lying down on his bed he twisted and turned but sleep was miles away. He did not want to think about that girl but the glimpses flooded his brain and took over his mind completely. She enjoyed life in very small things and this quality of her stands out. Rishi kept shifting sides but he was failing badly in achieving sleep. All he could think about was Aayat. He recalled her purple kurta and white leggings that she was wearing. Her hair were left open recklessly. The way she moved her fingers to tuck the hair behind her ears was something that made Rishi's heart skipped a beat. He loved her simplicity.

Us Nayi Nayi si Mohobbat mein Kitna saadapan tha. Dil ki har baat kitni saadah thi ... Saamne hokar bhi posheedah . Dil par kisi ki hukmrani thi Magar shartein nahi thi. Kitna Aasan tha Mohobbat kar Lena, kisi ki aankhon mein chipi udaasi Ko mehsoos kar lena, kisi ka Dard baant Lena. Ye Sab kitna Aasaan hua karta tha. Kam se Kam rishte kisi rang ke mohtaaj nahi the."

IX

Are You Inviting Me

She flipped the menu card placed right in front of her on the table. She was out that day with Zuly to their favorite cafe which was about two kilometers from their place. It was the first time they went out after their board examinations.

"When is the Holi party in your locality?" Aayat asked Zuly pretending to sound casual. Although Her nervousness was visible in the way she was pushing her micro nails into her skin as if she was planning a burglary. She already decided what she was going to wear for the party. She knew that the party got postponed a little bit because of the board exams of students. Moreover, what she was most excited about was that Rishi would be there. She remembered him from the last time at a similar party which was on New Year's Eve. She knew this time it was going to be more special. She has exchanged a few SMSs with Rishi in the last few days. She requested her mom to get her a msg card. They had a deal before her boards. Rishi was the first person she texted once she scratched the code and happily typed the digits on her relic Nokia mobile phone.

"it's probably this weekend, Sunday. You know how Sharma's uncle is. He makes sure that all the parties are done on Sundays only", Zuly said to Aayat moving the straw in her cold coffee.

The cafe was situated in the middle of a beautiful garden. It was famous amongst the youngsters. She loved going there. She was very particular about the table where she chose to sit. It's her favorite table near the windowpane where she can see the greenery outside. This was the place she chose to sit and think for hours.

Rishi was on her mind since the day she went to his place for asking about that set of problems. Zuly has been witnessing the growing curiosity in Aayat in the way she talked about Rishi. She was smart enough to understand that something was going on on both sides. Yet she was also very thoughtful to not ask Aayat about it directly. She was letting Aayat take her own sweet time before she admits something to Zuly. She wants her to surrender herself. Besides that, she has been keeping a keen eye on Rishi as well. She has seen Rishi smiling alone in his room simply by looking at his mobile screen and typing (God knows what). Zuly has been observing for quite a while now.

"You must come this time too. Rishi would be so happy" Zuly poked Aayat and looked straight into her eyes. She could see the color from her face disappear suddenly.

"What?? What do you mean?" Aayat Said brushing away the strand of hair from her eye. It was as if Zuly said exactly what she wanted to hear, not exactly from her but from someone else.

She was expecting the same reaction from Aayat. On the other hand, Aayat could feel her heart beating loudly inside her chest as if somebody has caught her kissing red-handed.

"I mean Rishi and You share such a nice bond. He would be so happy to see you there. You anyways be a part of all our society functions. You know what I mean right!", Zuly's words and her expressions weren't matching at all. She was saying genuine things and teasing her mildly.

"Yaa! Even I feel so. I'll talk to mom about it. Not that she is going to stop me. Now the exams are also over, and I have got nothing to do. A party this weekend won't be a bad option to consider you see" Aayat said. Pretending to be casual all the time. She had bad acting skills when she had to lie about something.

In the back of her mind, Aayat was planning what she was going to wear for the party. She had decided on the dress earlier, but the accessories were left.

"Hey! How about we go to the market? We have plenty of time before it's 6. So, I think I can probably get a good pair of earrings there. You know no, I need them for my dress." Aayat said smiling at her.

Zuly was smiling too just seeing Aayat getting so conscious about her dress, and her looks.

Is she the same Aayat Shaikh that I knew for the last 4 years? Zuly thought.

"Okay!! Let's go then". Zuly agreed to smile indefinitely. Aayat was so well versed with Zuly's expressions. Both looked at each other and smiled widely. They knew what they were smiling about, they knew that they both knew what was happening, but they let that little Mysterious hazy air survive between them.

Mysteries are a new cool.

"Titu bhaiyaa!! Bill le aaiye please" (Titu Bhiaya! Can you get us the bill!) Aayat shouted from her table. She was so excited about shopping for the party that she barely noticed those few faces in the cafe turning towards her.

"Are you mad! Why are you shouting" Zuly said slowly. "Everybody is looking towards us." She continued. Zuly could feel Aayat's excitement in her eyes.

"Sorry !!" Aayat said after noticing those few heads that just turned towards them.

They paid their bill and left.

Aayat was continuously talking during their entire rickshaw journey to the market.

"You know I don't want to take 'Jhumkis'. They'll not go with the dress. I think I should go for raindrop earrings. You know that dark silver-colored long, thin, and slender ones that we were looking for the other day, I want to have that." Aayat was talking continuously. She was anyways very fond of talking but the excitement in her eyes was new. Something which Zuly had never seen before. Yet when love starts thriving in, people in your surroundings just know it all. Even before you realize it within yourself. Aayat was a no different case. Zuly could feel that something was cooking inside which she certainly was unaware of.

"Watch this" Zuly said lifting a pair of earrings from the shop. Aayat was busy configuring where to start looking from. She came to the market, but she was pathetic at shopping and especially when she had to shop for accessories. She was confused with the array of earrings placed one after the other and covering the entire half of the wall. The uppermost line had all the Jhumkis then below that were lying the smaller ones, just in case you want the same design with a little less amount of weight. Furthermore, there were trendy sets too which you can wear on jeans. The salesperson in the shop was explaining which earrings they can wear with which dress. He seemed to contain so much information as if he tried them on.

He also told them which ones are going to get corroded soon if they meet water. Honest. Aayat was too busy with the designs to appreciate him.

"Noo Zuly. These are golden." Aayat said "I want that dark greyish earring with a leaf in the end. I loved it last time"

"It's not a textbook Aayat. Designs keep on changing. You can't just randomly move here and there in search of your dream earrings. It's been half an hour and we are nowhere. The deadline is still 6. And it's 5 already. You see we will take time to reach back too" Zuly talked rationally very rarely. But when she does, she meant it.

"Yaa I know. But then I can't invest my savings in something I'm not going to wear. I can't buy it just because I have to".

They left the shop and reached the last one in the lane. A cocktail of female colognes welcomed them in. Hush!

"Is there something on sale?" Zuly asked the shopkeeper who was, ironically, standing outside his shop.

"Yes. We have a whole new range of accessories. Hair bands, clips, perfumes whatever you want."

"Can you tell us if you have dark, greyish-colored earrings with a long slender chain and a leaf at the end? Only silver though" Zuly asked the shopkeeper straightforwardly. She knew there was no way they can enter this shop. And Aayat is not going to buy any other ones.

"I'll have to check madam". The shopkeeper replied and asked his assistant to look for the same design in the older lot. That Particular design that Aayat was looking for was last month's edition. She loved wearing what was out of fashion or older versions. That's a very special quality about her. When the world would move to new designs, she would be trying the older ones and be happy that she looked Different.

"This design is not the latest madam. You can look at the latest trends in our shop. You'll like it."

"No ... Please don't even try. This girl won't listen. If she wants that, she will have that only. Otherwise, she'll head back home, empty-handed". Zuly said sitting onto the chair placed outside. She was tired.

"I think you were looking for this!" The assistant came running and handed over the pair to Aayat. Aayat was extremely happy to see them.

"Finally!!! I got them..." Aayat was so happy with excitement and relief.

"Thank God!!! You got them...I was so exhausted...My God!!" Zuly said breathing in relief.

Aayat tried them on and looked in the mirror. She was happy. They paid the shopkeeper and left.

They reached back home at 6. Precisely, 7 minutes before it 6. It was still 3 days before the party but her mental calculations were wandering from what footwear she was going to wear to what dress she was going to put on, and most importantly, how is she going to start the conversation with him? Over texts, it's easier to talk but when the same person is in front of you, you just can't neglect the growing heartbeat.

Later, she texted Zuly in the night.

"I loved the earrings. They look amazing with the dress…"

Minutes later her phone beeped twice.

"Even if you wouldn't have got them, you would look amazing. Baby, Beauty lies in the eyes of the beholder. And you know that "beholder" admires simplicity"

Zuly texted back. Aayat was surprised by reading the text. She knew that Zuly was smart enough to notice everything but then these cryptic msgs were making Aayat a little shy. She has been so blunt all her life that now when she's blushing or feeling shy about something, it is so difficult for herself too to admit it.

"Someone was shopping today!!! Anything special !!"

Aayat opened the other text which was from Rishi

A big toothy smile filled her face with cheer.

How does Rishi know that I was shopping?? Did he see me struggling inside the shop?

Aayat was smiling madly over those six words text. It meant so much to her.

"Have you been following me!? How do you know??"

She typed back immediately.

Ohh!! What are best friends for? I'll see you Zuly.

Aayat thought. No one would have told him this. Zuly is the only link between them. And she knew Zuly was at his place. She lives in Rishi's house more than her own. Rishi's mother loved Zuly.

"Do I need to follow you to know about you!? Anyways u coming for the party right !?"

Rishi texted again.

There was a charm in opening up those envelopes and looking at text messages where you don't know what the other person has texted unless and until you open it.

That was a different space. She just loved them. Her old-fashioned phone gave her a little feel of classic letters. Nobody writes letters these days. Technology has killed paper-pen romance and long letters at the end of the week or a month. Aayat really to write letters, but she can't risk them coming into someone else's hands.

"Are u inviting me? ;-)" Aayat texted again.

"I don't think you need an invite. Everybody would be so happy to see u there."

Rishi was trying to be casually nice.

"Everybody or you ?"

Aayat texted back. She knew what she has said, and she knew the conversation was going to take a turn from that point.

They exchanged a few more msgs but then her phone's battery was going down. The conversation that has crept between them is way special for her. Love can make you do stupid things. The plug point was at the opposite end of her bed near the ground. She had to change the position of her pillow and plug in the charger. But the wire wasn't long enough. She lay half on the bed and half on the ground with her head going all the way to the ground. Her hair was touching the earth and gravity was making that conversation all the more difficult. Yet she laid there like that for about an hour after which Rishi said he had to go out.

Vikram was there. Vikram was Rishi's best friend. If anybody can make him do something outside his consent, that's Vikram. Vicky, as he called him.

Those three days before the Holi party were going to be so difficult to pass. Her heart was skipping a beat now and then just thinking about what the day would be like. There would be music, dance, food, and Rishi.

Smile has found a permanent place to live. Aayat's face was glowing with happiness.

Am I seriously blushing !!

It was so difficult for her to admit the fact that she was into an emotional connection that she had never experienced before. That Night was long, especially when she had to keep her phone aside as Rishi wasn't there.

In her mind, she had already started enjoining the party. More than anything she had started thinking about the time when Rishi would be around her and she would talk to him face to face. The day was awaited more than anything.

Only love can be so beautifully stupid.

She thought about Rishi and closed her eyes. Sleep was miles away.

Kisi ka intezaar, kisi ka khayal, kisi ki fikr kabhi kabhi kitni khoobsoorat ho sakti hai... Is baat ka Andaaza Insaan Ko tab hota jab wo kisi ke hone mein Apne aap Ko Dhoond le ... Kai khwab hum apni Haisiyat se upar dekh lete hain... Kai khwab itne khoobsoorat hote hain ki unhe Haqeeqat ki shakl Dena Mumkin nahi hota. Magar phir bhi hum Sab kuch bhool kar, har suljhi Hui baat se door Apne khwabon ka ek Aisa ghar banate hain jiska toot Jaana Tay hota hai ... Use Ta'ameer hote hue dekhna jitni Khushi deta hai, usse zada takleef tab Hoti hai jab wo Bina kisi theys ke khud ba khud toot jaata hai ... Aur Insaan itna majboor hota hai ki wo use bacha bhi nahi pata. Bas uske tukde samet-ta reh jaata hai ... Jinse phir dobara wo ghar kabhi nahi ban Sakta...

X

Strange Togetherness

A beautiful breezy evening arrived. Nobody has anticipated that. There was music at the party, half of the uncles and aunties were on the dance floor and mostly everyone was under the effect of 'Bhaang'. Rishi and Aayat have been together all through the day. There was a sense of calm, strange togetherness, even when there was nothing that had been accepted inside out. Yet what they were feeling is hard to describe. Later, Zuly and Vikram joined Aayat and Rishi.

Vikram noticed the growing redness on Aayat's face. He then placed a strong gaze at Rishi and realized that he too had the same expression. Vikram was an experienced man. He knew how to read faces. His experience told him that love had thrived. They are gone now.

"Mom had been calling me. I think I should leave now." Aayat said feebly gazing at Rishi.

"No ... Stay." Everybody just heard Rishi's strong voice echoing in the darkness of the windy evening.

Aayat, like a filmy heroine, instead of speaking, kept looking at Rishi with a strong will to resist the growing smile on her face. She couldn't.

"I have to go. It'll be very late otherwise". Somehow she managed to let her rational side speak.

"I'll drop you. Don't worry" Rishi didn't want her to leave. He was adamant.

Aayat noticed his intense eyes. Those dark caves beneath his eyes weren't letting her go. She knew she had lost herself, both in the argument and in Rishi's world. She continued staring at him. Chills ran down her spine.

"You two carry on. I'll catch up with you guys later." Vikram said and got up.

"Yaa! Even I am leaving. RJ, you drop her back home. Okay" Zuly said, and she too got up.

"Shall I drop you back?" Vikram asked Zuly. She nodded and began walking away from them.

Rishi knew he had to take Aayat somewhere before he bid her Bye. They got up from the grass and tapped their backs to let the grass fall off of their clothes. Aayat patted his back to remove the traces from it. Just a mere touch would ignite an intense feeling in Aayat. She had never been so close to a male identity.

"Shall we go?" Aayat said, adjusting her dupatta.

"After you ma'am!"

After walking a few meters, Aayat noticed that the route doesn't go to her house. She was talking to him and lost track of the route.

"This isn't the route to my home." Aayat sounded confused.

"Who said we're going to your place !!" She heard Rishi saying that.

"Where are we going then?" Aayat stopped midway on the road.

"Aayat! Do you trust me??"

She was silent for a few moments.

"I do."

"So just don't ask me now! I promise you'll be fine. You trust me no." Aayat answered with a smile.

Her phone beeped as she began moving again. She checked briefly. It was Zuly!

"Somebody's on a date! Yeah...I'm excited. Txt me once u reach home. I want the complete details. Xoxo: p"

Date?? It's not a date. Is it? Am I on a date? Like really? Oh my God!! No. I shouldn't be here. Relax Aayat. Stop overreacting. Rishi said

You'll be fine. Trust him.

The nervousness caused by Zuly's text was visible on her face. Minutes later, they reached the end of the road. She checked the time in her relic wristwatch, which her grandmother gave her. It was 7 PM. The sun had finally started settling down leaving only the orangish trails behind. There were no boundaries. Where the road ended was a turn, a bifurcation, where one side would lead you to one part of the city and the other side moved to the other end. It was a point where travelers have to decide their route for the further journey. They had to choose one to move ahead. On the other side, just before the cut, was a small tea stall, 'Tapri' as it was popularly called in Delhi. They were standing adjacent to the tea stall, where a Steel railing stopped them. Aayat grabbed it with both her hands and watched the remaining orange layers in the clouds, move into the darkness slowly.

"It's so beautiful ... I have never been here," Aayat said, mesmerized by the beauty that she was witnessing.

"Yes!! It is indeed beautiful. You know, Rishi said, "it's my favorite place. I always come here alone. This is the first time I have come here with someone. Not even my friends know about it ."

Aayat suddenly felt so special.

"Really!? Thank you!! You know I have never really seen Delhi like this ... Even it's my first time too."

Rishi moved closer to Aayat.

"I had spent months here, just standing and watching the sun going below the horizon. You know Aayat, Rishi continued, "for months, I have cried here remembering her. I still do. I have cried till my eyes hurt. But She never came back."

"What??" She was stunned for a while. She couldn't keep the shock inside.

"Are you talking about some girl?" She continued.

He nodded. "I don't know Aayat. It's been 3 years since she's gone. She never said anything, she never explained the reason why she was leaving me. You know, there was a time when I used to cry all night. In the morning I would find my pillow to be so wet. I had to hide it because I didn't want my mom to be worried. My family knows nothing about her. She was a part of me. When she left, I had nothing to live for. I don't know how I have survived up till now. I just don't know. I don't know why I am telling all this to you. I'm sorry".

Rishi was speaking out his heart for the first time. Aayat had never seen him talk so much. When today, he was talking, Aayat did not judge him at all. She left a part of her heart empty so that whatever Rishi wants to dump out of his heart, she can keep it inside hers, safe. Aayat had always noticed Rishi's sad eyes, yet she was unaware of the reasons. Today, she was feeling happy to finally learn the reason.

"Aayat, I had never been able to throw her out of my heart. She continued to live in me even when she wasn't there."

There was a moment of silence. Only his wavy breath was audible. One side of his face was visible to Aayat as Rishi was staring into oblivion.

"Rishi!" Aayat called his name. "Look at me."

Like an obedient child, he looked at Aayat. She noticed his eyelashes. It appeared as if somebody has sprinkled morning dew over them. Even in the moistness, they looked beautiful to Aayat.

Aayat placed her palm on his cheek. Her fingers began moving from his cheeks to his nose and finally wiped away the last drop of tear from the corners of his eyes. She kept caressing his face. It was a moment none of them was anticipating.

Rishi Gujral just cried in front of Aayat Shaikh.

"If she left you without even telling you the reason, she was not worth it Rishi. She never loved you. Stop punishing yourself for the things she never did for you. Let it go. It's high time you get her out of if four minds." Aayat knew she has got the least persuasive skills. Yet, she tried her best.

"Rishi ... I don't know who she was. I also don't know why she left you, but you know what! I can only tell you this whoever is going to be with you, that girl would be very lucky. The kind of struggle that I have seen in your life, I know you're born for bigger things. I can feel it Rishi...You are born to win the skies. Your struggle and your strength inspire me. It makes me understand the true worth of life. Whenever I see you, I feel you're way above everyone because being the youngest, you have supported your family. Have I been had in your shoes; I would have been shattered by now. Just because a girl left you, doesn't mean you were to be blamed for things. She probably left because she either fell out of love with you or never fell for you ."

Aayat's words echoed in his ears and a strong rush of tears began flowing from his eyes. Rishi could barely control himself. He pressed his lips tightly to not let the sighs spill out of his mouth.

"Rishiiiiii ..." Aayat took his name and immediately hugged him.

For the first time, they did what they were feeling for the last so many days. She held Rishi like a small baby. She was a few inches shorter than Rishi. Rishi had to bend a little to completely bury himself in her arms.

On Onn unknown evening, on the roadside, where the sun was falling quickly as the dusk was mingling with the night, they were sharing a moment that none of them is going to forget. Several vehicles passed by them at full speed yet the embrace were unbreakable.

They separated after a few minutes.

Aayat wiped his tears with her fingers and kissed his moist eyes. She didn't think twice before doing it. It just felt right.

Rishi was taken aback. He placed his eyes on her face. A roadside lamp had been illuminating their faces as the darkness was increasing, slowly.

Both went silent for a while. Nobody had anything to speak about.

"Would you not ask me who was that girl ...?" It was Rishi's voice to break the silence.

"Jis baat se aapko takleemain, main uska Bhiam Bhi Nahi Lena chahti ... Aap ne Mujhe Itna Bata Diya hai, mere liye Wahi bohot hai ... Mein hu aapke Saath ... Hamesha." (Things that hurt you, I don't want to even talk about it. You've told me so much, that's enough for me. I am always with you.")

"You trust me so much?" Rishi asked her with a feeble smile on his face.

"Yes, Rishi...I do"

She smiled.

Aayat poured some water on his hands and Rishi washed his face.

Rishi pulled her dupatta and stood straight in front of her. Drops of water were moving down from his face to his neck and finally settled on his chest. His bare chest was visible a little from the upper two buttons which he always leaves open. He lifted the dupatta and wiped his face with it.

Aayat was laughing at his gestures.

"Chai piyogi...!!?" (Want to have some tea?) Rishi asked her.

"Yeah! Sure" she replied briefly.

"You'll have the best tea of your life today," Rishi said and asked the tea vendor to get them two cups of tea.

"They serve it in 'Kulhads'. You'll love it." Rishi said and smiled widely.

"I'm already loving it." Her smile was pointing to a lot of other things than just a cup of tea.

They shared their first cup of tea. She had never thought of being in a place like that. Those moments were very special for her. She had witnessed a lot of things that she had never witnessed before. There was a subtle serenity that you can only feel with certain people.

"This is so amazing!! How do they make it." Aayat said with the first sip of it.

"I told you !"

They sat on a little platform that was there. Just sitting on the roadside under the lampshade could be so beautiful. They had forgotten completely that they had to go back home.

"Shall we go now?" Aayat said looking at her watch. "It's 8 already. We'll take time to go back too."

"Why do you want to run away?? Always in a rush to go back!! Huh!" Rishi said, annoyed.

"I'm not in a rush Rishi!! It's just that mom would be waiting for me.

She told me to be back by 9. If I'll be a minute late by 9, she will kill me.

"Tumhari mummy hain ya Angrezon ke zamane ki jailor?" Rishi said and they both laughed.

"Oh My God!! Rishiiiiii !!"

Aayat said and continued laughing.

"So!! When are you coming out with me next time?" Rishi asked straight.

"Do I have to? Really?" She said in a mocking voice.

"Ahaan!!??"

"Ahaaaannn", She said.

As she started walking away from him, Rishi grabbed her wrist. She looked back in amazement.

The place bears witness to what he said.

"I know you understand everything. Even those things which I never said but I feel I had to tell you this..." Rishi said.

"Aayat Shaikh! I Love You..."

Aayat froze for a while. She couldn't believe her ears. She was taken aback.

She knew they were moving close to it but she didn't know she'll hear it so soon.

"I love you too Rishi Gujral ..."

As she said that, she found herself buried in his arms. They hugged each other as if they were so hungry. Hungry, to be loved. Their restlessness fell off completely. They were serene. They were complete. It was magic that has cast a spell on them. They knew their lives are going to be changed completely. They knew their names were different. Too different to be written together.

"I don't know what's gonna happen next. I have never thought about the future. But I promise I'll be with you as long as I can. I don't know about anything. I don't know whether it's right or wrong. I don't know what your religion is. Right now, I want you in my life. You make me happy Aayat. You have inspired me so much. I don't want to be away from you." Rishi said while embracing Aayat.

Aayat tasted her tears. She knew love was knocking at her door for a long time now, but she never anticipated it to come her way as it did.

In the back of her mind, she was aware of the difference in their names. She understood the difference between saffron and green and unfortunately, she knew these two colors can never be mingled in this world. Yet what she was feeling was so strong that she kept the uncertainties aside for a while and lived in the moment.

The tea stall vendor was looking at them and smiling. He had been friends with Rishi for the last three years. It was the first time he was watching Rishi in a completely different light.

"Chotu!! Kishore Sahab ki ghazlein Laga de Aaj… Mujhe lagta hai Barish hone wali hai…" (Chotu! Plugin Kishore Kumar's cassette today. I think it's going to rain)

He said and smiled for a little longer.

Rishi heard the song "Pyaar Deewana Hota hai" playing nearby. He saw the tea stall vendor, Radheshyam, smiling from a distance.

Rishi blushed for the first time that evening.

Aayat looked at Rishi and then at Radheshyam. She smiled widely.

Rishi sang the song along with the tape recorder.

"Shama kahe parwane se, pare chala Jaa

Meri tarha jal Jaayega yahan nahi aa…

Wo nahi sunta usko jal Jaana hota hai

Har Khushi Se har Gham se beghana Hota hai…

Pyaar deewana hota hai mastaana hota hai,

Har Khushi Se har Gham se beghana Hota hai…"

Rishi held Aayat's hands and kissed them.

Rishi was blushing for the first time, Aayat's cheeks had gone red and most importantly, Radheshyam was smiling too.

It was a perfect evening. He played a few more songs before they finally left.

It had started raining …

"…Jab kabhi Mohobbat kisi se Ki jaaye, Apne Sab sawalon Ko kahin dafan kar aaya jaaye … Yaqeen hi bohot hona chahiye ek naye rishte ki shuruaat ke liye

... Yaqeen ... Itna bada lafz ho jata hai ki kabhi kabhi Mohobbat Jaisi paak cheez bhi uska bojh Sambhal nahi paati ... Wo dheh jaati hai, kisi be-buniyaad imaarat ki tarha. Bharosa sambhale rakhna har ek Mohobbat ki Qismat mein nahi hota ..."

AUTHORS NOTE

will be continued...?
     Dear Readers,
I hope you've enjoyed reading it just the way I've enjoyed writing it.
I would love to know how you find it. :))
     Love
Aadesh!!

STAY CONNECTED WITH US

https://Aadesh27.blogspot.com/
https://www.instagram.com/positive__chhora/
Dubey_aadesh@yahoo.com